BILL GATES

Gloria D. Miklowitz

ᴘ Dominie Press, Inc.

Publisher: Raymond Yuen
Editor: John S. F. Graham
Designer: Greg DiGenti
Photo Credits: Doug Wilson/Corbis (Page 7);
AFP/Corbis (cover and pages 16, 23, and 27)

Text copyright © 2002 Gloria D. Miklowitz

All rights reserved. No part of this publication may be reproduced or transmitted in any form or by any means without permission in writing from the publisher. Reproduction of any part of this book, through photocopy, recording, or any electronic or mechanical retrieval system, without the written permission of the publisher, is an infringement of the copyright law.

Published by:

Dominie Press, Inc.
1949 Kellogg Avenue
Carlsbad, California 92008 USA

www.dominie.com

Paperback ISBN 0-7685-1214-X
Library Bound Edition ISBN 0-7685-1539-4
Printed in Singapore by PH Productions Pte Ltd
  4 5 6   09 08 07 06

Table of Contents

Chapter 1
Strong-willed, Intelligent, Competitive 5

Chapter 2
C-Cubed 10

Chapter 3
BASIC 14

Chapter 4
MS-DOS 20

Chapter 5
Windows 26

Glossary 35

Chapter 1

Strong-willed, Intelligent, Competitive

Bill Gates is the man behind Microsoft, the company every computer user knows. When he was born on October 28, 1955, only huge computers existed. They were slow, very expensive, difficult to use, and few companies or universities could afford them. From the age of twelve, when Bill first became aware what a computer could do, he was fascinated. As computer design improved, he and his best friend, Paul Allen, found ways for computers to do things that weren't possible before.

William H. "Bill" Gates III grew up in Seattle, Washington with his sisters, Kristi and Libby. Bill's father was a lawyer. His mother taught school until he was born, then did volunteer work as he grew up.

From his earliest years, Bill showed great intelligence and curiosity. When he was only eight, he read everything in the World Book Encyclopedia up to the letter P. He spoke like an adult, and people knew him as a math and science whiz. He had a remarkable memory, and was able to memorize pages of text

Bill Gates, in his mid-twenties, at Microsoft headquarters in Redmond, Washington

with a quick look. At school he got A's in almost every class.

The Gates children were encouraged to ask questions and discuss things. Bill loved to argue, so much so that his parents were worried. They sent him to a psychiatrist who told them what they already guessed, that he was strong-willed, very intelligent, and very competitive.

Mr. & Mrs. Gates believed their very bright son needed new challenges. So, after sixth grade, they enrolled him at Lakeside School in Seattle. It was an expensive private school with very high standards. There, in 1967, the school became one of the first in the country to introduce computers to their students. With $3,000 raised by school mothers, Lakeside bought time for their students on a computer owned by General Electric, linked by telephone lines to the school.

From the day Bill discovered computers and what they could do, he was hooked.

Chapter 2
C-Cubed

Only twelve years old, Bill, and friends Paul Allen and Kent Evans, cut classes to spend time in the computer room. They went back at night to play with the machine and learn everything it could do. Bill discovered how to play tic-tac-toe and Monopoly on the computer. Within weeks, the three boys used up most of the time the school had paid for.

Soon their school contracted for student time with Computer Center Corporation (which Bill called C-Cubed). The new computer was more complex. The boys loved working on it and sometimes caused it to crash or fail. C-Cubed offered them free time on their computers if they would look for and describe the failures and other bugs. They filled nearly 300 pages documenting those bugs.

Seeing the possibilities for making money with their knowledge, they formed the Lakeside Programming Group. Their first job was to arrange their school's class schedule. They earned nearly $4,000 for a summer's work. When C-Cubed went out of business in 1970, they were hired by Information Sciences, Inc. to create a payroll program for its computer.

Then, tragedy struck. Kent Evans died in a mountain climbing accident. Bill and Paul Allen grieved for their friend but carried on together, forming the company Traf-O-Data. They developed a program for the computer to count holes punched in cards, measuring traffic. Traf-O-Data earned $20,000 in its first year of business.

When he was seventeen, Bill went to Washington D.C. for the summer as a congressional page. Even there he saw ways to make money. He bought buttons from the losing McGovern-Eagleton presidential campaign for a nickel each. Then he sold them as collector's items for up to $25 each. Bill told a schoolmate he expected to be a millionaire by the time he was 25.

Still in high school, Bill's company was offered a job. TRW, a company with military contracts, wanted them to find ways "to crash its system" so they could correct the problems. Despite working almost full time for TRW, Bill graduated from high school in the Spring of 1973.

In the fall, he went to Harvard University to study pre-law. In his two years at Harvard, Bill spent more time in the Computer Lab and playing cards with friends than he did in the classroom.

Then something happened that decided the rest of his life.

Chapter 3
BASIC

One day, Paul Allen saw a copy of the January 1975 issue of Popular Electronics. On its cover was a picture of the Altair 8800, the first build-it-yourself personal computer kit. He immediately called Bill. The two had talked often about starting a company to write software for computers. If computers could be small enough for personal use, almost everyone could own one. If so, those computers would need software—the set of instructions that tells them how to operate.

Bill phoned the company that had invented the Altair, MITS, located in Albuquerque, New Mexico. Bill told them he had a new form of the programming language BASIC, which had been around for a while. He could deliver it within weeks. The truth was that he had no program at all. But he was sure he could create one.

Paul tried to make the Harvard computers act like the Altair so he and Bill could test the new program. Then

Bill Gates speaking to a crowd about the Windows operating system

Bill started work redesigning BASIC for the Altair. He stopped playing cards. He even stopped attending classes. For the next eight weeks, the two young men worked day and night. They often slept on the floor of the computer lab and grabbed fast food when they were hungry.

In late February, Paul flew to Albuquerque with the new BASIC program. He acted confident but felt unsure. Bill's version of BASIC worked on the computers at Harvard. But would it work on a real Altair?

MITS (Micro Instrumentation & Telemetry Systems, Inc.) was a low-budget company, nothing what Paul expected. The day after he arrived, he loaded the BASIC program into their Altair and crossed his fingers. Suddenly, the machine came to life.

Paul keyed in, *Print 2+2*.

The Altair printed *4*.

"These guys were really stunned to see their computer work," Paul said. "I was pretty stunned, myself."

When Paul returned to Boston, he and Bill celebrated by going out for ice cream and sodas. There was a lot of work to be done, but they knew they could do it.

In the next few months, Paul worked at MITS and Bill returned to classes to finish his second year at Harvard. But by summer, Bill had made up his mind. Despite his parents' objections, he left college. His future, he believed, was with computers.

That summer, not yet twenty years old, Bill formed Microsoft (short for "micro-computer software"). Bill and Paul were on their way to becoming millionaires.

Chapter 4
MS-DOS

Soon, however, MITS was in trouble. Problems with the hardware led to lower sales. Bill and Paul became concerned that their software might be associated with a bad product.

Many new computer companies were springing up, among them Apple, Radio Shack, and Commodore. In an attempt to keep up with the competition, MITS agreed to be sold to another company who wanted to make computers and distribute Microsoft's version of BASIC with them.

But Bill knew that if he let his software be given over to another company he would lose control of it, and his business would be over. Microsoft sued both companies over control of BASIC and won.

Soon, Bill and Paul predicted, people all over the world would want personal computers for many different uses. They would need software to do bookkeeping, to write letters and other documents, play games, and much more. Microsoft would have to expand to fill those needs.

By late 1978, Bill moved Microsoft to where he grew up, near Seattle, Washington. The first new people they hired were some of his high school computer buddies. They were kids with long hair who wore jeans and T-shirts, not shirts and ties like other companies at the time.

Earlier, in 1975, the computer giant IBM tried to produce its own personal computer, but it was a failure. IBM was making huge computers, called *mainframes*, for big companies and government agencies. But they knew that personal computers were part of the future.

They decided to try producing a

Bill Gates in front of a sign showing the number days until release of a new version of Windows

personal computer again in 1980. But this time they wanted to make sure it would succeed. The software that ran on IBM's mainframe computers wouldn't work with the smaller, newer personal computers. So they needed to find someone who could write the right kind of software and sell it to them. They decided to hire Microsoft.

Bill told IBM that he had the right software for them. He didn't really have the software, but he knew how he could get his hands on it. He knew of a company called Seattle Computer Products (SCP), whose owner had invented a system called SCP-DOS (Disk Operating System). SCP didn't know IBM was looking for such a system. Bill bought SCP-DOS from SCP for $50,000 and renamed it MS-DOS. Then he licensed MS-DOS to IBM.

By licensing it instead of selling it, Microsoft would get money whenever IBM sold one of its personal computers that ran MS-DOS. This way, if IBM's personal computer was a big success, Microsoft would share in the success.

IBM's Personal Computer (PC) sold very well, and MS-DOS became very popular. There were other DOS-type programs at the time, but MS-DOS eventually became the leader.

Chapter 5

Windows

The next big leap in Microsoft's history came with the development of Windows. In the 1970s, a computer research company, Xerox, developed a kind of computer system that no one had ever seen before, called *Alto*. It had a graphical screen, a mouse, and could show the user how text would look when it was printed out. Bill visited Xerox and saw this computer.

So did a company called Apple. When the Apple Computer Company developed their new computer, the Macintosh (most people call it the *Mac*), Bill was asked to write software for it.

The Mac used a different operating system from MS-DOS. For MS-DOS, a user needed to know a few hundred commands. By contrast, Mac users saw pictures, called icons, on their screens, showing what the computer could do. A user points and clicks on an icon instead of having to remember and type in the commands each time. This is called GUI (Graphical User Interface) computing. This was the same type of system that was developed at Xerox.

In 1984, Microsoft came out with Windows. It was a new operating system using icons, like the Mac. Many people dismissed Windows and the Macintosh. How could they be powerful enough to run the newer computers if they were so easy to use?

But Windows became more and more popular, and soon people saw what it could do. More and more people could buy computers because the software was so easy to use. Windows did the same things that DOS did, but in a way that was easier for people to understand.

Meanwhile, Apple's Macintosh wasn't selling as well. Windows computers could run the old DOS programs, but the Mac couldn't. People had to buy all new software if they wanted to switch from DOS to Mac. Also, Apple insisted on selling their own computers with their software. Microsoft only sold software, leaving other companies to sell the hardware, which was often much more inexpensive than Macintoshes. People could buy cheaper computers that ran Windows software, and it didn't matter who made the computers.

In 1988, Apple decided to sue Microsoft because Windows behaved the same way as a Mac. They said that Microsoft copied the Mac "look and feel." But Bill argued that both Windows and Mac systems borrowed different features from Xerox's Alto computer. Because Xerox had decided not to sell its computer system, the "look and feel" of it could be used by anybody. Bill won the lawsuit and kept selling Windows to more and more people and companies.

By the time Microsoft was ten years old, it had over 1,000 employees and was selling all kinds of software, including Windows. There were offices in Latin America, Europe, Asia, and Mexico. Bill, at 31 years old, was a billionaire.

But the Windows operating system wasn't selling well, even when an improved version was introduced in 1987. Most people used MS-DOS or Macintosh as their operating systems.

Bill decided to change all that. In 1990, Microsoft came out with

Windows 3.0, which added more features and fixed problems with earlier versions. This version of Windows sold very well. People started using Windows more and more.

By the time Windows 95 came out in 1995, Windows 3.1 and MS-DOS were already running over 120 million computers worldwide. He also made sure that companies which built and sold computers had Windows software ready to run when customers bought them.

Concerned that Microsoft was unfairly dominating its rivals, the Federal Trade Commission stepped in. They questioned Bill and other Microsoft employees, but ruled finally that they weren't doing anything wrong. This would not be the end of questions about Microsoft's methods.

Every year, Microsoft has improved Windows and added new software such as the computer encyclopedia Encarta, and the browser Internet Explorer. Microsoft has grown so large now that its headquarters occupy 49 buildings on 29 acres.

In 1994, Bill married Melinda French after six years of dating. They now have two children, a girl and boy, and live in a huge, completely computerized home near Seattle.

In addition to being advocates for education, donating millions each year, the Gates family became concerned by the terrible conditions of the world's poor. They learned that one of every five children die in Mozambique, Africa before the age of five. In addition, they learned that people in some countries don't live past the age of 50.

To help change this situation, they created the Bill and Melinda Gates Foundation, the largest and best-funded foundation in history. Run by Gates'

Bill and Melinda Gates

father, its purpose is to help the world's poor through education, better health care, and research into deadly diseases. By 2002, the foundation was worth about $25 billion.

Bill Gates fell in love with the computer as a twelve-year-old. Through innovation and hard work, he built Microsoft Corporation, a company that has changed our lives and the lives of future generations.

Glossary

Advocate - someone who supports and acts in favor of something.

Agencies - organizations that are in charge of something.

Albuquerque - a large city in New Mexico.

Arrange - to move things around so they look or work better.

Association - an organized group of people or companies that have something in common.

BASIC - stands for Beginners All-purpose Symbolic Instruction Code. A computer language that uses English words as commands.

Billionaire - a person who has a billion or more dollars.

Bookkeeping - keeping track of money.

Boston - the capital of Massachusetts.

Build-it-yourself - something you buy that you have to put together.

Campaign - in politics, a strategy for someone to run for public office.

Commands - codes that tell a computer what to do. see *Instructions*

Commission - an amount of money that a salesperson gets as a reward for selling something.

Contract - a legal agreement between two people or groups that says what both must do for each other.

Development - when a person or group is building something and figuring out how it should work.

Dismiss - to think something isn't useful or valuable enough to try it out.

Dominate - to be better or more successful than others, sometimes by putting them down.

DOS - stands for Disk Operating System. It was the first type of system software to run personal computers.

Electronic - a type of machine that uses the movement of electricity through special parts to make it work.

Eventually - something will happen if given enough time.

Federal - having to do with the United States government.

Genius - someone who is very smart.

Hardware - the physical part of a computer. It can also refer to different pieces of a computer.

Harvard - a university in Massachusetts; part of the "Ivy League." It is the oldest university in the United States.

Headquarters - the main area of a company or organization.

Imitating - copying; doing the same things.

Instructions - in computers, the codes that tell a computer what to do. see *Commands*

Interface - the way a person can give a computer instructions.

Keyed - typed.

Latin America - Central and South America.

Licensing - letting someone else sell your product.

Mainframe - a type of large computer many businesses used to use in the 1970s and 1980s.

Mozambique - a large country in southeast Africa.

Occupy - to take up or fill a space.

Payroll - the money that companies pay their employees.

Pre-Law - a set of classes that people take to prepare for law school.

Program - in computers, an arrangement of codes, or instructions, that tells a computer to do something. see *Software*

Psychiatrist - a kind of doctor who deals with mental and emotional problems.

Redesigning - making something different, usually so it works or looks better.

Software - programs that can run on a computer.

Version - one kind of something; something that is a little different from the original.

Volunteer - working without being paid, usually for a good cause.